The Life of *Ralph*

ISBN 979-8-89428-361-6 (paperback)
ISBN 979-8-89428-362-3 (digital)

Christian Faith Publishing
832 Park Avenue
Meadville, PA 16335
www.christianfaithpublishing.com

Printed in the United States of America

The Life of *Ralph*

Loraine Brady

What a beautiful day for Ralph to take a nap on the rug at the front door!

Today Ralph is wearing his orange sweater and his blue shoes.

This morning, a big black dog came up to the
fence, and Ralph was watching him.

The children in the schoolyard were playing with Ralph.

Ralph spends a lot of time lying on his back enjoying the sunshine.

Ralph is in trouble because he tore up Mrs. Rain's flower bed.

Ralph has decided to go play in this mud puddle today.

Ralph saw a woman riding a bicycle down the
sidewalk, and he started running beside her.

Today, Ralph is just sitting around watching
the red birds play in the flower bed.

Ralph was hot from running around the yard, so he decided
to splash the water out of his bowl to cool off.

This morning, Ralph went to school to play with the children. The teacher called and told me to come get Ralph because the children wanted to go play with him.

He is just taking in the sunshine today.

Ralph is playing in the swimming pool with his friend Ducky.

Ralph is running down the sidewalk so he
could find someone to play with.

Ralph is on a fishing trip with Mrs. Rain and Rodney.

Ralph is dragging his cover out of the doghouse.

Today Ralph is playing hide-and-seek in the river canes.

Ralph had spotted a hen, so he broke the henhouse
door open and started chasing my chickens.
I just happened to see him, and I ran out there and
was yelling for him to get out of their pen.

Ralph is having to take a bath in this large tub this
evening because he got all muddy today.

Ralph is digging his way out from under the
fence so he can go see Toddles.

This evening, Ralph was playing in the yard, and he spotted
a squirrel. Then suddenly he decided he wanted to chase
after it, but the squirrel ran up the tree really fast.

Ralph has decided to jump in the pond, and
he is trying to catch my ducks.

Today Ralph ran fast, chasing a cat out of the yard.

Today he got in trouble for being out of the yard and running the streets.

Ralph is hiding under the porch because he
fears the thunder and lightning.

Ralph and Toddles are hanging out on the porch together today.

It's a very cold and snowy day, but Ralph is
really having fun playing in the snow.

Mrs. Rain put some dog food in Ralph's bowl, and
he didn't like it, so he pushed it away.

A storm was blowing in. Ralph got scared, and
he ran inside the house to hide.

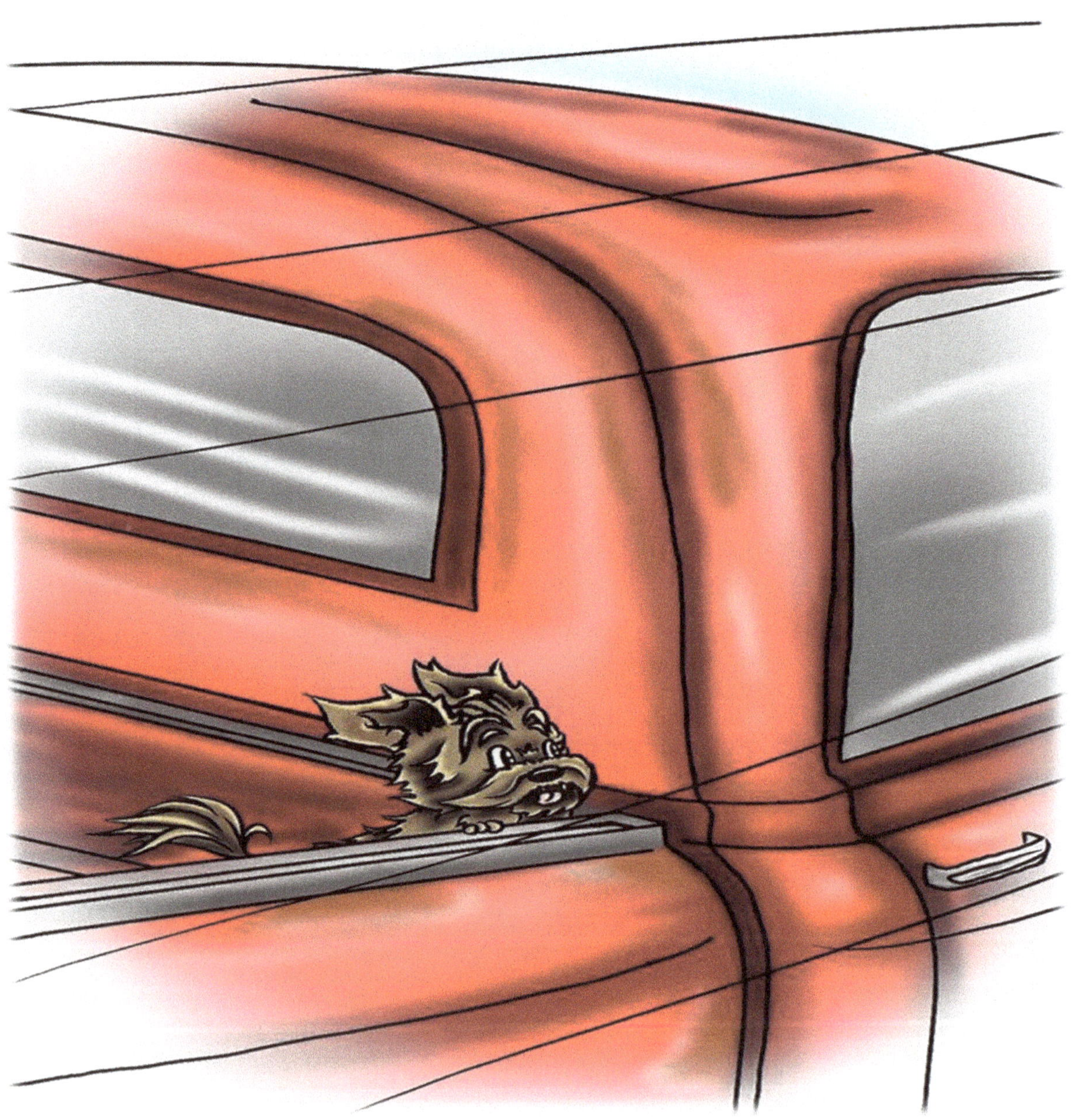

It was a day for Ralph to get a ride in the back of our little red truck.

In the evening, Ralph would go over to the
little store, and he would get a treat.

Ralph

Mrs. Rain's Dog

About the Author

My name is Loraine Brady

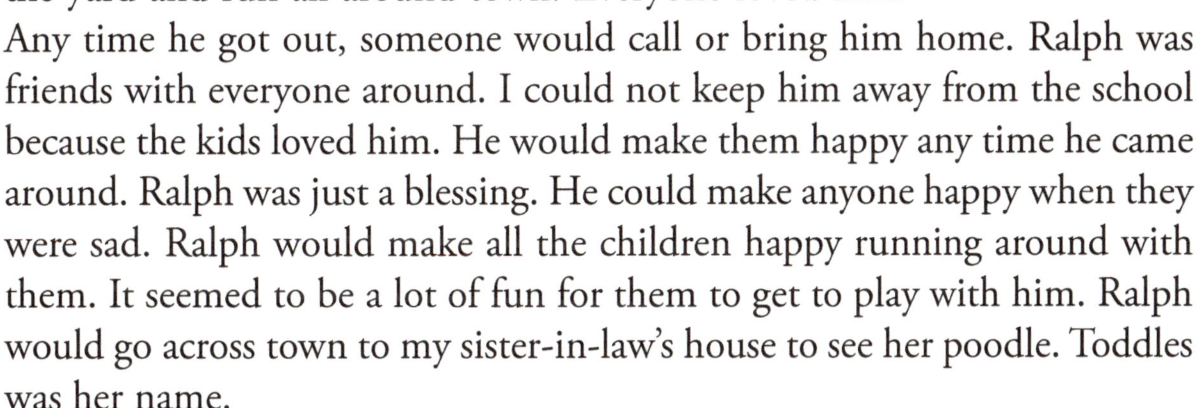

I just want to talk a little about the purpose of this book.

This book is based on a true story of my dog and a small town.

My dog's name was Ralph. He was a short red-haired dog. Ralph was a gift from my son.

He could run very fast, and he would sneak out of the yard and run all around town. Everyone loved him. Any time he got out, someone would call or bring him home. Ralph was friends with everyone around. I could not keep him away from the school because the kids loved him. He would make them happy any time he came around. Ralph was just a blessing. He could make anyone happy when they were sad. Ralph would make all the children happy running around with them. It seemed to be a lot of fun for them to get to play with him. Ralph would go across town to my sister-in-law's house to see her poodle. Toddles was her name.

My husband and I really loved Ralph. He was just like our child. We spent a lot of time with him. The police office would bring him home sometimes when he got out. To keep Ralph from digging out from under the fence we had to tie a rope to his collar and, on the other end, a milk jug so that he couldn't get under the fence, but that did not last. He still got out. Later in the years, Ralph accidentally got ran over, and that just broke everyone's heart.

So the reason I want this book is to give everyone a memory of him to keep. He was in everyone's heart and was loved so much. I want to keep his memory alive, and we all still talk about him today. Every time I see a dog that looks like him, I get so sad. I just miss him so much.

I really need this book published because the children who grew up with him can tell their children all about Ralph. This is a story that will never die in this little town. Ralph is buried in my front yard and will always be in our lives, not just as a memory but in our hearts. When you read the book, you will understand my feelings with this beloved dog. I will never be able to replace Ralph because he was one of a kind. I do not want to make my book sad, but I do want to make it a memory book.

Sincerely,
Loraine Brady